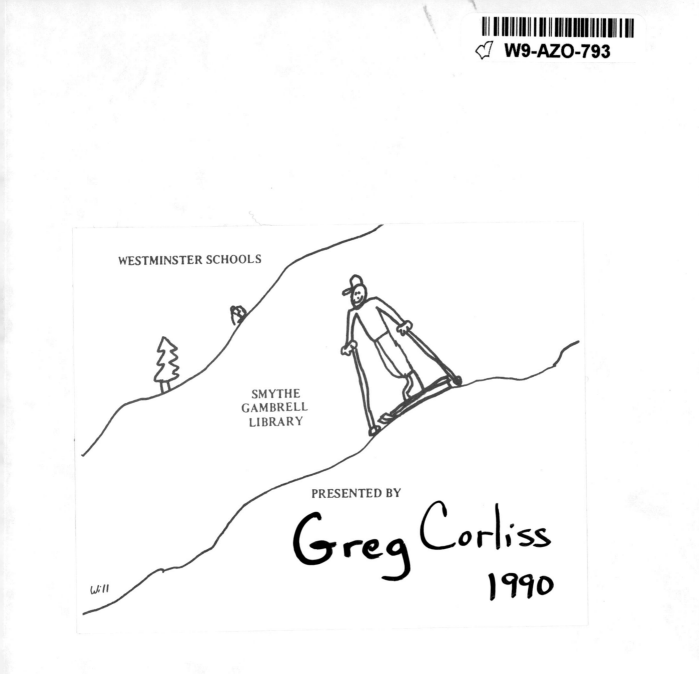

WESTMINSTER SCHOOLS

SMYTHE
GAMBRELL
LIBRARY

PRESENTED BY

Greg Corliss
1990

Will

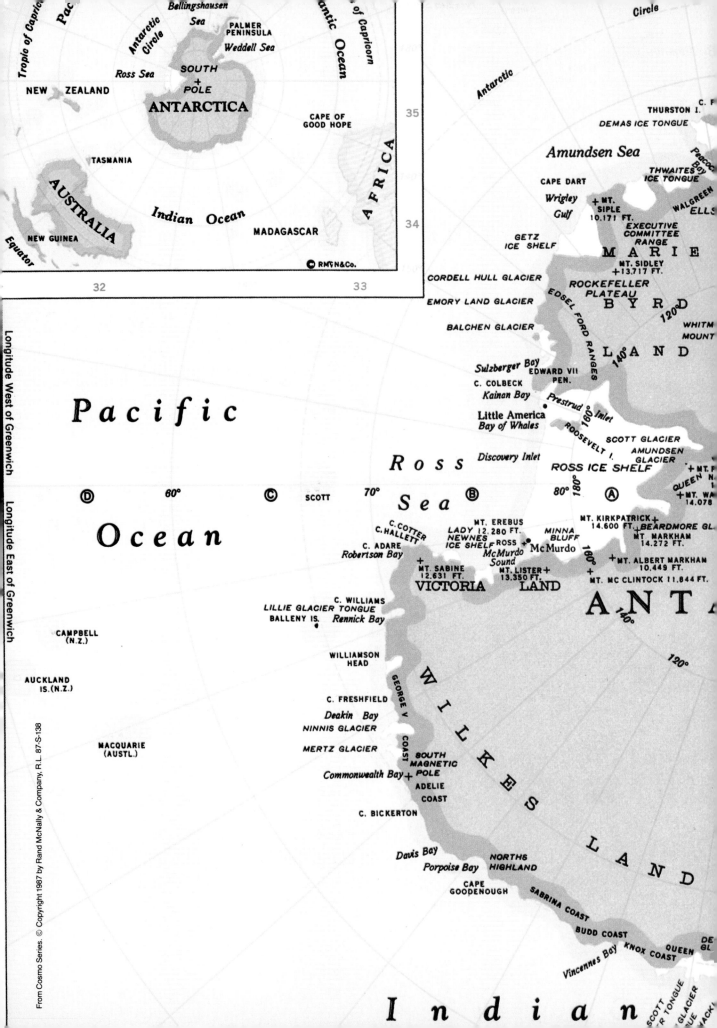

Inset Map (upper left)

Tropic of Capricorn

Pac... Ocean of Capricorn

Bellinghausen
Sea

PALMER
PENINSULA

Antarctic
Circle

Weddell Sea

Ross Sea

SOUTH
+ POLE

ANTARCTICA

CAPE OF
GOOD HOPE

AFRICA

NEW ZEALAND

TASMANIA

AUSTRALIA

Indian Ocean

MADAGASCAR

NEW GUINEA

Equator

© RM'N&Co.

35
34
32
33

Main Map

Pacific

Ocean

Ross

Sea

Antarctic Circle

THURSTON I.

DEMAS ICE TONGUE

Amundsen Sea

Peacock Bay

THWAITES
ICE TONGUE

WALGREEN

CAPE DART

Wrigley
Gulf

+ MT.
SIPLE
10,171 FT.

EXECUTIVE
COMMITTEE
RANGE

ELLS

GETZ
ICE SHELF

MT. SIDLEY
+ 13,717 FT.

MARIE

CORDELL HULL GLACIER

ROCKEFELLER
PLATEAU

BYRD

EMORY LAND GLACIER

EDSEL FORD RANGES

120°

WHITM

BALCHEN GLACIER

LAND

140°

MOUNT

Sulzberger Bay

EDWARD VII
PEN.

C. COLBECK

Kainan Bay

160°

Prestrud Inlet

ROOSEVELT I.

SCOTT GLACIER

AMUNDSEN
GLACIER

Little America
Bay of Whales

Discovery Inlet

ROSS ICE SHELF

80°

180°

A

+ MT. F
QUEEN N I
+ MT. WA
14,078

60°

C

SCOTT

70°

B

MT. KIRKPATRICK
14,600 FT.

+ BEARDMORE GL.

MT. MARKHAM
14,272 FT.

C. COTTER
C. HALLETT

MT. EREBUS
LADY 12,280 FT.
NEWNES
ICE SHELF

MINNA
BLUFF

160°

C. ADARE

Robertson Bay

ROSS + McMurdo

McMurdo
Sound

+ MT. ALBERT MARKHAM
10,449 FT.

D

MT. SABINE
12,631 FT.

MT. LISTER +
13,350 FT.

MT. MC CLINTOCK 11,844 FT.

VICTORIA

LAND

ANTA

CAMPBELL
(N.Z.)

C. WILLIAMS
TONGUE

LILLIE GLACIER
BALLENY IS.

Rennick Bay

140°

WILLIAMSON
HEAD

GEORGE V

120°

AUCKLAND
IS.(N.Z.)

C. FRESHFIELD

Deakin Bay

NINNIS GLACIER

COAST

MACQUARIE
(AUSTL.)

MERTZ GLACIER

SOUTH
MAGNETIC
POLE

WILKES

Commonwealth Bay +

ADELIE
COAST

C. BICKERTON

LAND

Davis Bay

NORTHS
HIGHLAND

Porpoise Bay

CAPE
GOODENOUGH

SABRINA COAST

BUDD COAST

DE
GL

SCOTT TONGUE

QUEEN

KNOX COAST

Vincennes Bay

JACK

Indian

DESTINATION:
ANTARCTICA

by ROBERT SWAN

photographs by Roger Mear, Robert Swan, and Rebecca Ward

SCHOLASTIC
HARDCOVER

SCHOLASTIC INC. / *New York*

Library of Congress Cataloging-in-Publication Data
Swan, Robert.
Destination Antarctica.
Summary: Follows the British adventurer Robert Swan
and two other explorers on an exciting and dangerous
900-mile trek to the South Pole.
1. Mear, Roger—Juvenile literature.   2. Swan,
Robert—Juvenile literature.   3. Scott, Robert Falcon,
1868–1912—Juvenile literature.   4. Antarctic region—
Discovery and exploration—Juvenile literature.
[1. Swan, Robert.   2. Antarctic regions.   3. Explorers]
I. Title.
G850 1985.M4S93   1988   919.8′904   87-20793
ISBN 0-590-41285-X

12 11 10 9 8 7 6 5 4 3 2   9/8 0 1 2 3/9

Printed in the U.S.A.   23

First Scholastic printing, February 1988

I would like to thank
Barry Denenberg for his invaluable help
in the preparation of this book.
—R.S.

Preface

IT WAS spring of 1912. Robert Scott and his companions had been expected back eight months earlier.

Scott and his party had set out to be the first men to reach the South Pole. At the time, the way to reach the South Pole was on foot, sometimes with the help of dogs, through nearly nine hundred miles of ice, wind, and snow. It was a long and dangerous trek through the frozen continent of Antarctica.

On January 17, 1912, Scott and his party finally did reach the South Pole, only to find a Norwegian flag planted by Roald Amundsen. Scott's team arrived five weeks too late.

Several months later, the eleven-man search team came upon a mound of snow. "It is the tent," said one of the men. They dug out the tent and discovered the bodies of Bowers, Wilson, and Scott wrapped in their reindeer-skin sleeping bags.

Next to Scott was a tin with a lamp wick, which he probably used for light when he made entries into his diary. The last entry was on March 29:

> Since the twenty-first, we have had a continuous gale from the west southwest and the southwest. We had fuel to make two cups of tea apiece and have food for two days on the twentieth. Every day, we have been ready to start for our depot eleven miles away, but outside the door of our tent, it remains a scene of whirling drift. I do not think we can hope for any better things now.

The search team collapsed the tent over the bodies and built an eight-foot mound of snow; they made a cross out of a ski.

"This must last for many years," said one of the search team. But the monument was never seen again. Sun and snow would cause it to sink beneath the surface, where the bodies, preserved by the snow, will remain until one day an iceberg breaks from the edge and carries them north.

Seventy-four years after Scott began his final expedition, Roger Mear, Gareth Wood, and I, Robert Swan, embarked on a trek dedicated to Scott's memory. Without the help of animals, machines, or radios, we manhauled food, gear, and supplies over the same route Scott took. Our expedition was named "In the Footsteps of Scott," and this is our story.

Men Wanted for Hazardous Journey

FOR AS long as I can remember, I have enjoyed studying history. I like learning about other places and times. Even more, I am fascinated by individuals and what they accomplished.

To tell the truth, though, something always bothered me. I didn't want to spend my whole life reading about things that other people did. I wanted to do them myself. It was that simple. I wanted to *write* history, not read it.

One day, when I was twenty-one, I was spending a long morning in the library at the University of Durham. I had been in the ancient history stacks for hours when I wandered to a section on polar exploration. I pulled out one of the books, opened it, and was attracted by an extraordinary photograph. It was of the men who were with Captain Robert Scott on his tragic journey to the South Pole. The look in their eyes made an impression on me. I decided right then that I wanted to experience what they had experienced. I wanted to go where they had gone, do what they had done, and see what they had seen. I decided I would do whatever I had to. I was going to the South Pole.

From that time forward, my life was different. I felt excitement and anticipation. I knew I had lots to do, and I began immediately. I started by reading books about the history of the exploration of Antarctica: about Scott and his gallant crew; about Ernest Shackleton, another British polar explorer; and about Roald Amundsen.

I decided I really needed to experience Antarctica firsthand before I could begin to make preparations for the expedition. So in 1979, I presented myself at the Cambridge offices of the British Antarctic Survey, which maintained a year-round base of operations in Antarctica in a place called Rothera. I told them that I wanted to join them at Rothera. I asked them how I could make myself useful there, and they told me.

For a year and a half, I worked at one job after another, learning the various trades that the people at BAS told me were important. I learned to fix motors, mend machines, climb mountains, and mix concrete. In September 1980, I returned to the same BAS offices and soon was on my way to Rothera Base, Antarctica.

On the trip, I got to know Roger Mear, whom I had met earlier at a BAS conference. Roger was already recognized as one of a handful of world-class mountaineers. His still-growing list of firsts included successful challenges of the world's highest and most forbidding mountains. Roger usually chose to scale their sheerest slopes, often in winter and sometimes in darkness. He was more at ease facing step-by-step dangers on an icy mountainside than strolling to the corner store for the Sunday paper. I was sure that this was the person I wanted in charge in Antarctica.

At first, to use his word, he was "under-whelmed" with the idea. After careful consideration he agreed, but with one provision: that we did it his way. "We must make a one-way journey to the Pole together yet alone. Without depots, dogs, or outside assistance of any kind. We will not take radios or rescue beacons. We will start with as much food and fuel as we can haul, and once past the halfway mark, it will be the South Pole or nothing."

After our stay in Rothera, Roger returned to his mountaineering life and studied the particular techniques we would need to cope in the Antarctic. I returned to England in 1981, when I set out to gather what was needed for the expedition: people, food, equipment, money, a ship.

I decided to run the ad that Ernest Shackleton had run in a newspaper over seventy years ago when he, too, was planning an attempt to reach the Pole:

> Men wanted for hazardous journey. Small wages, bitter cold, long months of complete boredom, constant danger, safe return doubtful. Honor and recognition in case of success.

Thanks to the Shackleton ad and stories about the expedition that appeared in newspapers and occasionally on television, we received over four thousand applications. From those, and from people whom Roger and I knew, we chose the twenty-five members of our expedition. All would make the boat trip to Antarctica, though only Roger and I planned to walk to the South Pole.

Gareth Wood, a thirty-four-year-old Canadian, was among the twenty-five. Roger had climbed with him many times. Gareth had left his life on rural Vancouver Island to organize all aspects of our base. Gareth's courteous manner seemed to be a good balance to my natural brashness and Roger's closed-book personality.

Gareth was a welcome and critical addition to the team, as was Michael Stroud, whom Roger and I met on our trip to Rothera Base. Michael was to be our doctor, assuring us of proper medical care. Dr. Michael would be able to combine two things he enjoyed: adventure and medicine.

Though our ad stated "Men wanted," we had three women among the crew, including Rebecca Ward, who joined our team as a photographer.

John Tolson, a thoughtful person who has a tendency to reserve judgment, became our cameraman, shooting over twenty-six hours of film that would become a fifty-two minute documentary of our journey.

We set up operations in a warehouse located in Shed 14 on the London docks. It was just yards away from where Scott's ship, the *Terra Nova*, was loaded. Now that we had a warehouse, we needed to fill it. I planned to ask men and women who ran companies for money and supplies, and I put together a presentation for that purpose.

Sir Peter Scott, Robert Scott's son and cofounder of the World Wildlife Fund International, is widely respected by conservationists. In early 1982, he gave us his full support. As I had suspected, it made things quite a bit easier. Companies would listen to me with Sir Peter Scott's support.

We soon began to make headway. We received assurances from Shell that they would supply our fuel. Rolex supplied our watches; Leica, our cameras; Bow Water-Scott, our toilet paper. Before we would set foot on the continent of Antarctica, we would raise three and a half million dollars in money and supplies that represented the good wishes of over two thousand companies, schools, and individuals.

My friend Peter Malcolm joined us in search of a ship that was capable of navigating the icy and treacherous Antarctic seas (or could be made capable) and also within our budget. Peter found a gleaming red and white vessel that we later named the *Southern Quest* after Shackleton's ship, the *Quest.*

At the end of March 1984, the ship accidentally crashed into the wharfside London docks, scattering bricks, wood, and the welcoming party in all directions. I tried to see it as a good omen. "That, Ladies and Gentlemen, was a demonstration of her ice-breaking capabilities."

It took nine months of professional refurbishing to insure that the *Southern Quest* was in condition for the hazardous journey. Finally, on November 10 at nine o'clock in the morning, preparations came to an end. With a small group of friends and well-wishers bidding us farewell, we set sail for Antarctica. My dream was becoming a reality.

Bound for Antarctica

THE ROUTE of the *Southern Quest* followed Captain Scott's: from London to Cardiff, where we picked up sixteen tons of coal (as Scott had), then on to Cape Town, South Africa.

Lyttelton, New Zealand, was our last port of call before Antarctica. We set sail on January 30 after a two-week stay. We were escorted through the still waters of the channel by the tug *Lyttelton*, which had escorted Scott's ship, *Terra Nova*, seventy-four years earlier.

Five days later, we passed through some of the roughest seas in the world. We entered waters that were 36°F. There were icebergs and snow.

On February 7, we sighted Mt. Erebus, the active volcano. It seemed to keep watch over the Antarctic landscape.

All of us were aware of the problems that could be caused by the unpredictable waters of McMurdo Sound. A ship might pass through unharmed at one point, only to be immobilized in pack ice at the next, frozen solid for a year or more.

When we finally landed, we had little time for rejoicing or resting. The Antarctic summer was ending, and the pack ice that had let us in was already reforming. We had no time to spare.

Gareth supervised setting up the base. He went about his job with the precision and preparation that we had come to expect. Twenty-five of us took eight 15-hour days to unload the cargo, all fifty tons of it.

Our evenings were spent eating and enjoying each other's company. Resting our tired bones, we moved as little as possible.

Gareth's plans were well thought out, and we were able to erect our hut, which came in pre-fabricated sections, in only four days. We named our base after Sir Jack Hayward, one of our sponsors.

Scott's hut stood two hundred yards from our base. Clothes, boots, socks left for drying, books, and photographs of loved ones remained where they had been when abandoned three quarters of a century earlier. The food and fuel that Scott had so desperately needed was still there in its original abundance.

Over the past eight years, I had studied the photographs of Scott and his men. Now, standing where they had spent so many hours, I felt their presence. The sound of my boots on the floorboards startled me. For a moment I thought one of Scott's men was there, about to ask just what in the world I was doing and who I was.

I returned to our hut and lay awake for quite a while thinking about what we were going to attempt and about those who had gone before us.

Antarctica has few plants and animals. Microscopic life, moss, lichens, tiny wingless insects, and two types of flowering plants live on the land. Penguins, seals, and the skua (a bird) also inhabit the continent, but they spend only part of the time on land. These animals depend upon the sea for their food.

A small human population of mostly research scientists also lives in Antarctica. The scientists are from several nations that have agreed to share their discoveries.

McMurdo, an American base, is heated and lighted by a small power plant. People, supplies, and mail are transported by airplane.

A Long Wait

THE SUN doesn't appear at all for four months during the height of the Antarctic winter; the weather is brutal.

We arrived in Antarctica at a time when the *Southern Quest* could enter McMurdo Sound. Now Roger and I had to wait until the following summer, when the sun would return and the weather become milder, to walk to the South Pole. Gareth Wood, Dr. Michael Stroud, and John Tolson waited out the nine months with us. Meanwhile, Dr. Michael did medical research, and John filmed our activities.

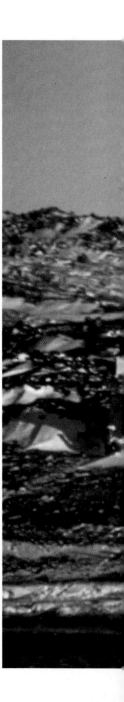

The temperature had been dropping almost daily since we arrived. The Antarctic winter was approaching. On February 23, the *Southern Quest* departed for the warmth of Sydney, Australia, where she would spend the winter. Roger, Gareth, Michael, John, and I stood at the shoreline and watched the others disappear across the bay. The five of us would spend the next nine months together in a space that measured sixteen by twenty-four feet.

We entered our hut through a porch, where we kept coal, skis, and sleds. Just inside the door was the bathroom/storeroom. The toilet used biodegradable chemicals, and the contents were emptied into the sea each day.

We kept most of our food outside, but food to be used in the next few days and food that could not be frozen was in the pantry. Our living room contained a coal-burning cooker that doubled as a heater, a dining room table, a kitchen sink, and water tanks for melting blocks of snow thrown in through a hatch from outside.

There was also space for Gareth's radio equipment, a computer that was kind enough to play chess with Roger, Dr. Mike's medical equipment, and a darkroom for developing film. Our bedrooms were upstairs in an atticlike space below the roof.

The most critical feature upstairs was the window that opened in case of fire. Outside, we erected a tent, stocked with emergency supplies as a precaution.

Fire is the single greatest hazard to huts in Antarctica, where it never rains and rarely snows. A piece of dry wood could be ignited by the smallest flame, and strong winds spread a fire. A dropped fuel can and a match carelessly tossed away could mean sudden and total disaster.

Antarctica forces you to think about everything you do. The extreme cold, the driving and relentless wind, and the foreign terrain will make you pay for any lapse in concentration.

Winter in Antarctica brings many extremes: temperatures that fall to −70°F and lower, winds that reach over a hundred miles an hour, terrain that is without life and appears forever frozen solid. But perhaps the most trying extreme is when the sun deserts the continent from the middle of May until the last days of July. During that time, only the moon lights up the sky.

It was interesting to watch everyone develop schedules for eating, sleeping, and working in a sunless environment. I preferred taking cat naps. I often woke at four in the morning and usually read until seven or so. Then I began my chores: burning the rubbish (we were committed to leaving the continent as unlittered as we found it), bringing in blocks of snow for drinking water, emptying the latrine. I also wrote many letters to people who were interested in our progress.

Roger never seemed to sleep at all. Staying up all night, he pored over his charts and maps and made certain that our plans for navigation were correct. Gareth kept to a more normal schedule.

I don't recall exactly when the tensions began to build, but by May it was clear that our original plan would not work. The problems that Roger and I encountered with each other's personalities caused enough distrust between the two of us to make a two-man walk dangerous. Choosing a third to join us was the only way to proceed. A third would relieve the tension and balance things out. There was little question that Gareth Wood was the most qualified to join us.

The South Pole or Nothing

W E SPENT the days before our trek calculating, weighing, and repacking our food. We did everything we could to reduce the weight. We even unwrapped 480 chocolate bars to save 26 ounces. But no matter what we did, we could not get our sleds to weigh less than 353 pounds. My sled turned out to weigh .2 pounds less than Gareth's and Roger's. Discovering this, Gareth said that they would let me get away with it this time.

John and Mike walked with us for fifteen miles from our base to Hut Point. They left us to begin our journey from Hut Point on November 3, the same location and day that marked the beginning of Scott's expedition. We were scheduled to arrive within eighty-three days. We had food for no more.

We didn't push ourselves those first few days. We knew that no matter how well-conditioned we were, it was best to let our bodies gradually get used to the shock of this kind of load. But somewhere along the way, we would have to make up for our slow initial pace in order to average the ten miles a day that were essential to cover the distance.

The wind blew from the south directly into our faces. The surface was very difficult. By day ten, we had traveled only 86 miles, an average of 8.6 miles a day. It was not good enough, so we pushed on.

But at least by now, we could no longer look back and see where we had come from.

We slept right next to each other, head to foot, in a small tent. Each morning, we were up at seven. Gareth, who slept in the middle, was the first to rise. The moment I opened my eyes, I felt as if I hadn't slept enough the night before.

There was barely enough room for us to sleep in the tent. Moving and putting on socks and shoes was even more difficult. Dressing was quite a gymnastic exercise. Though it was very cold, I couldn't dress too rapidly. Dressing for the day could actually mean the difference between life and death. It would certainly mean the difference between comfort and discomfort during the day's walk. I had to carefully apply antiperspirant to my feet to prevent sweating. Moisture in my shoes would freeze and give me frostbite. A wrinkle in a sock could cause a blister that would get worse every day. If I put on too much clothing, I would have to stop, take off the extra layer, and repack my sled. Then I would have to make up the time that I had lost.

After a quick breakfast of hot chocolate, oatmeal, biscuits and butter, we broke camp and were on our way. We would walk for three hours, rest for ten minutes, walk for three hours, rest for ten minutes, walk for three hours. During our rests, we would have a snack of chocolate and salami. After our last period of walking, we would set up camp and eat a freeze-dried dinner.

Each day, one of us would take a turn supplying the food we needed from his sled. This would make the sled six pounds lighter. It felt great every time my turn came. We carried our trash with us because we did not want to add to the pollution of Antarctica.

We were always hungry and often bored. To pass the time, I would pretend that the walk from one campsite to another was a stroll across London. One day I would walk from Hampstead Heath to Euston Station. Another day, I would walk from the Barbican to Westminster Abbey. I would try to remember every landmark and feature along the way. My problem was that I would also picture every restaurant, cafe, and food shop. I always finished my stroll hungrier than ever.

At night, it was all we could do to fight off exhaustion so that we could light our tiny portable stove and fix dinner. After dinner, Roger and Gareth worked on the navigation tables for the next day's march. Staying on course was one of our major concerns.

We carried only one book with us, Scott's diary. Each night, we would read the entry from the corresponding day of Scott's journey. Although sleep beckoned, we always took time to write in our own diaries.

Our first major obstacle was the four-hundred-mile Ross Ice Shelf, an immense plane of floating ice covered with ice ridges, crevasses (deep cracks), and snow crusts that could suddenly cave in from our weight. On skis, we pulled our sleds, each man lost in his own world. Each decided for himself when to stop to take a breather or adjust clothing or equipment. The slowest would catch up when it was time to set up camp.

The wind blew from the south at twenty-five miles straight into our faces. It did not let up. Spinning particles of frozen snow made it difficult to see and hear.

I was consistently falling behind. By the twenty-fifth day, I had fallen a full mile behind. Roger came to see if he could help. He pulled my sled and discovered it was harder to pull than his. After some investigation, Roger discovered the problem. The runners were on backwards. The difference was not apparent to the naked eye, but in

Antarctica, the most minute mistake could bring defeat or even death. Roger took the runners off and turned them around, and we were on our way.

After thirty-eight days and three hundred ninety-seven miles, we reached the end of the Ross Ice Shelf. Now we were ready to face the most dangerous terrain on the entire journey: the Beardmore Glacier. It was a nine-thousand-foot climb over a distance of one hundred thirty-six miles, with a surface of rugged ice covered by waves three and four feet across.

But in spite of the dangers, the Beardmore was a welcome sight. It symbolized the progress we had made. It meant there was a great deal behind us.

At the halfway point Roger, Gareth, and I had an important decision to make. If we chose to continue beyond this point, there would be no turning back. We had enough food and supplies to turn around *or* to continue to the South Pole; we did not have enough to turn back at a later date.

The decision was unanimous. It would be the South Pole—or nothing.

Roger saw them first: the tents, the helicopter, and the men. When I got closer, I took off my goggles and blinked to make sure that my eyes were not deceiving me. They were not. Four American geologists and one Russian scientist were surveying the area. They invited us to join them for an extravagant dinner of lobster and steak, and we accepted. The next day we rested, suffering from too much food and feeling disappointed that things had not gone as originally planned: that we would face the same challenges, including the same isolation, that Scott and his men had faced. We had not expected to meet other people until we had reached the Pole.

It happened on our forty-third day: what I had feared since the beginning of our journey. On December 15, I had an accident. My sled swung out of control and trapped my foot in a crack in the ice. The ligaments in my knee snapped as I fell. We still had four hundred seventy-one miles to go.

"You'll just have to go on at your own pace," said Roger. "Do your best, and we'll never separate too far from you. But we can't slow up at this point."

I agreed. My knee swelled within just a few hours, but I could still walk on it.

Though it took me longer, somehow I managed to cover the daily mileage. Every night, I caught up with my partners while they were setting up camp.

In spite of my injury, we scaled the Beardmore in only seven days, five days less than it took Scott and his party. I quoted the words John Mills spoke in the movie *Scott of the Antarctic*: "Barrier done. Glacier done. Plateau ahead."

We had less than three hundred fifty miles to go once we reached the Polar Plateau, an ice-covered flat surface at an altitude of ten thousand feet. The surface was smoother now, allowing us to return to our skis, but the wind once again blew directly into our faces. We feared that it would get worse and that blizzards would halt our progress. Navigation was becoming a critical problem nearly every step of the way. Roger continued to navigate in circumstances that seemed impossible.

Our bodies were sapped dry, and I could feel that I had dropped as much as thirty pounds. Our lips were cracked with vertical lines of blood, and there were circles around our eye sockets from our goggles.

We were drained mentally as well. I found myself talking to people who weren't there. I would have daydreams about sitting in a restaurant with people all around me eating sumptuous feasts—but no waiter would come to my table. My mind filled with nonsense as my imagination traveled to distant planets.

The terrain grew worse as we encountered sastrugi, windblown waves in the snow. To our weary minds, they seemed like an endless chain of mountains that had to be climbed one by one.

On January 10, we were only 11.27 miles from the Pole. By the next day, we were 8.79 miles away, but visibility had become so bad that Roger could no longer be sure that we were on course. We had to stop. The winds that night blew at thirty-six miles an hour, the strongest winds recorded since 1958. Fortunately, the blizzard lasted only a few hours, and we were marching once again, each thinking about the Pole, which was now within reach.

I thought I spied something, but I wasn't sure. I continued hopefully. It became clearer. It was the geodesic dome that capped the Amundsen-Scott South Pole Station. We were five days earlier than planned, and there was no one to be seen. Then I noticed movement. A hooded figure motioned for us to follow him. We went down the ramp that tracked vehicles used to go in and out of the station. We walked under a sign that read, "The United States Welcomes You to the South Pole." It was eleven fifty-three at night.

The manager of the station shook my hand. Gripping his, I felt overwhelmed by the knowledge that we had done it. We had reached the South Pole, following in the footsteps of Scott.

Epilogue

B UT ALSO like Scott and his party, disappointment would greet us at our moment of victory. After our handshake, the manager of the station quickly informed us of the disaster that had occurred only hours before. "Welcome," he said. "I'm glad you guys made it. I've got some bad news for you, though. The *Southern Quest* has sunk. It was crushed by pack ice. Fortunately, everyone is safe."

The *Southern Quest* had spent the winter in Sydney, Australia. In preparation for the trip south, the crew dismantled a small Cessna aircraft and loaded it on board. The plane was to fly us directly from the American base at the South Pole back to the *Southern Quest.*

On January 9, 1986, the *Southern Quest* encountered pack ice. The captain, Graham Phipper, decided there was little choice other than to look for an ice flow that was large enough to allow the crew to assemble the Cessna. An ice flow was found, but the pack ice continued to be a threat. The ship drifted with the ice. By January 11, it was clear they were stuck. All hands chopped ice and did what they could to free the ship. It was a gallant but hopeless effort. The ship was trapped and slowly crushed. Rivets popped; decks buckled. She went down slowly at first, then the process speeded up. The bold white letters spelling *Southern Quest* disappeared one by one, and she was completely engulfed.

I arranged for the crew of the *Southern Quest* to be flown to New Zealand. Roger and I joined them. Gareth Wood and two members of the crew volunteered to stay in the hut for the next year until I could arrange to clear the beach as originally planned. In December 1986, the three volunteers were picked up by a small twin-engine Otter aircraft. In February 1987, the hut and remaining supplies were taken away by ship, completing the expedition.

Though time has put a distance between me and the expedition, every day is filled with memories, both good and bad: the excitement during our many years of preparation; the thrill of the boat trip; the tensions that we felt in the hut during that brutal Antarctic winter; the great hunger, bitter cold, and frightening injuries that we endured during our trek; our first disappointment, our encounter with the scientists; our joy as we reached the South Pole; and our greater disappointment, the sinking of our ship.

We had experienced all that. And we had lived up to the epitaph of Scott and his men, a quote from Tennyson's "Ulysses": "To strive, to seek, to find, and not to yield."

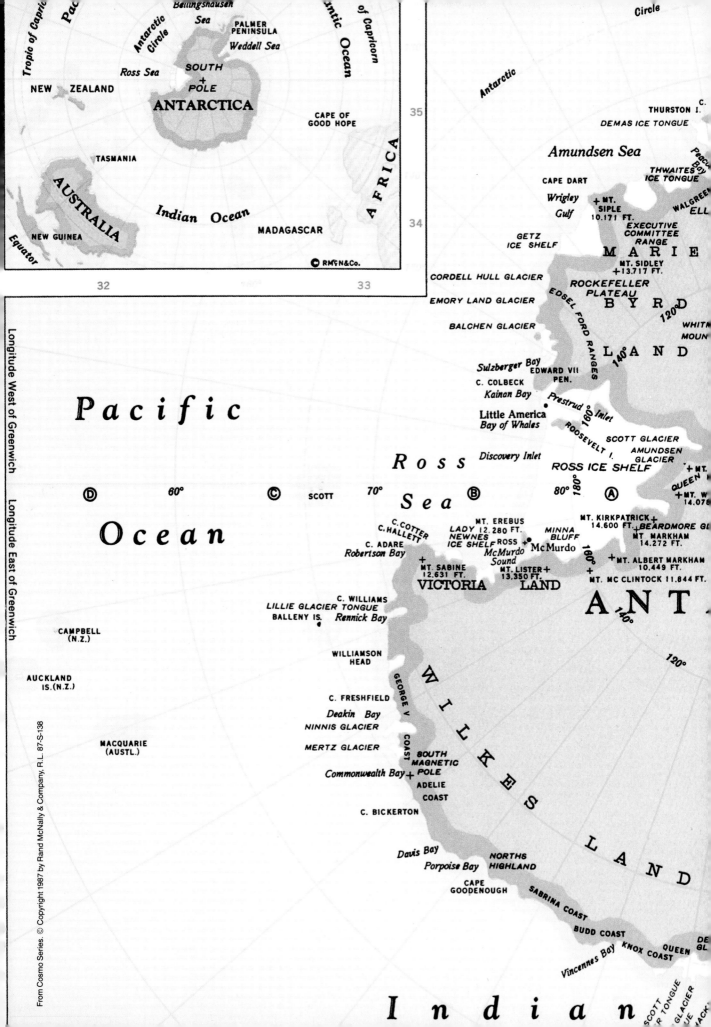

Inset Map (top left)

Tropic of Capricorn

Pac...

Bellingshausen Sea

of Capricorn

...ntic Ocean

Antarctic Circle

Antarctic Circle

PALMER PENINSULA

Weddell Sea

Ross Sea

SOUTH + POLE

ANTARCTICA

NEW ZEALAND

CAPE OF GOOD HOPE

35

34

AFRICA

TASMANIA

AUSTRALIA

NEW GUINEA

Indian Ocean

MADAGASCAR

Equator

© RM&N & Co.

32   33

Main Map

Antarctic

Circle

THURSTON I.

DEMAS ICE TONGUE

Amundsen Sea

CAPE DART

Peac...

THWAITES ICE TONGUE

Bay

Wrigley Gulf

+ MT. SIPLE 10.171 FT.

WALGREEN

ELL

GETZ ICE SHELF

EXECUTIVE COMMITTEE RANGE

M A R I E

MT. SIDLEY +13.717 FT.

CORDELL HULL GLACIER

ROCKEFELLER PLATEAU

B Y R D

EMORY LAND GLACIER

EDSEL FORD RANGES

120°

WHITN MOUN

BALCHEN GLACIER

L A N D

140°

Sulzberger Bay

EDWARD VII PEN.

C. COLBECK

Kainan Bay

Prestrud Inlet

180°

Little America

Bay of Whales

ROOSEVELT I.

SCOTT GLACIER

AMUNDSEN GLACIER

Discovery Inlet

ROSS ICE SHELF

+ MT.

QUEEN

80°

180°

+ MT. W 14.078

Pacific

R o s s

SCOTT

70°

S e a

B

A

MT. KIRKPATRICK 14.600 FT.

+ BEARDMORE GL

D

60°

C

MT. MARKHAM 14.272 FT.

MT. EREBUS 12.280 FT.

LADY NEWNES ICE SHELF

ROSS

MINNA BLUFF

C. COTTER

C. HALLETT

McMurdo Sound

McMurdo

C. ADARE

180°

+ MT. ALBERT MARKHAM 10.449 FT.

Robertson Bay

+ MT. SABINE 12.631 FT.

MT. LISTER 13.350 FT. +

MT. MC CLINTOCK 11.844 FT.

Ocean

VICTORIA LAND

A N T.

C. WILLIAMS

LILLIE GLACIER TONGUE

BALLENY IS.

Rennick Bay

140°

CAMPBELL (N.Z.)

WILLIAMSON HEAD

120°

AUCKLAND IS.(N.Z.)

C. FRESHFIELD

Deakin Bay

NINNIS GLACIER

GEORGE V COAST

W

MACQUARIE (AUSTL.)

MERTZ GLACIER

Commonwealth Bay +

SOUTH MAGNETIC POLE

I

ADELIE COAST

L

C. BICKERTON

K

Davis Bay

NORTHS HIGHLAND

E

Porpoise Bay

CAPE GOODENOUGH

SABRINA COAST

S

L A N D

BUDD COAST

DE GL

Vincennes Bay

KNOX COAST

QUEEN

SCOTT TONGUE GLACIER

I n d i a n